You Don't Say!

Tongue Twisters, Perverse Proverbs and Foot-in-Mouth Disease

Aubrey Malone

Copyright © 2017 Aubrey Malone

All rights reserved, including the right to reproduce this book, or portions thereof in any form. No part of this text may be reproduced, transmitted, downloaded, decompiled, reverse engineered, or stored, in any form or introduced into any information storage and retrieval system, in any form or by any means, whether electronic or mechanical without the express written permission of the author.

ISBN: 978-1-326-98900-2

CONTENTS

Introduction

Re-inventing the Language 2

It's the Way You Tell 'Em 16

Generally Speaking 30

Things You Should Know 43

Truths Universally Acknowledged 55

Are We Missing Something Here? 68

Run That By Me Again 79

That's Not The Way I Heard It 88

Introduction

We don't always get it right when we open our mouths. In fact some of us seem to open them only to change feet.

Prince Charles, who would know about such things, has coined the term 'Dontopadology' to describe such an affliction. Many people before him – most notably Sir Boyle Roche and Sam Goldwyn - were exponents of it. But there were many other less-known foot-in-mouth merchants. Football pundits seem particularly prone to it, and indeed sporting people in general. One could nearly compile a whole book of Murray Hill's clangers.

The bottom line is that nobody knows what they're going to say until they say it. After they do, it's too late to take it back.

Thankfully, for the purposes of this book, even Nomer hods.

Re-inventing the Language

Long dresses cover a multitude of shins. (**Mae West**)

Don't let the cat out of the bag after the barn door is locked. (**Honey Flexer**)

I thank you from the heart of my bottom. (**Nick Faldo**)

Hindsight is always 50/50. (**Bertie Ahern**)

Don't bite the hand that lays the golden egg. (**Sam Goldwyn**)

An Englishman's home is his hassle. (**Paul Arnold**)

I'm drawing a line under the sand. (**John Major**)

The earth shall inherit the meek. (**Dave Allen**)

I may be dumb but I'm not stupid. (**Terry Bradshaw**)

Comedy is no laughing matter. (**Richard Whateley**)

Those who can, do. Those who can't, teach. And those who can't teach become PE instructors. (**Woody Allen**)

Bureaucracy defends the status quo long after the quo has lost its status. (**Laurence J. Peter**)

Marriages are made in heaven. But so is thunder and lightning. (**Clint Eastwood**)

A Freudian slip is when you say one thing and mean your mother. (**Jackie Mason**)

One man's Mede is another man's Persian. (**George S. Kaufman**)

Two heads are better than one unless they're on the same body. (**Tony Hancock**)

If you're there before it's over you're on time. (**Jimmy Walker**)

My philosophy of women is wine, women and so long. (**Dean Martin**)

Genghis Khan but Immanuel Kant. (**Simon Carmody**)

Jeffrey Archer is forgotten but not gone. (**Hugh Leonard**)

Blondes don't necessarily prefer gentlemen. (**Mamie van Doren**)

The world will end not with a banger but a Wimpy. (**Graffiti**)

If music be the food of love, why are so many romantics tone deaf? (**Dave Allen**)

Don't put Descartes before De Horse. (**Sean Kenny**)

In America you're guilty until proven wealthy. (**Bill Maher**)

The shortest distance between two points of view is a straight lie. (**Bette Davis**)

The quality of Mersey is not strained. (**John Lennon**)

I was born with a silver spoon in my foot. (**George Best**)

McDonalds ensures the survival of the fattest. (**Stephen Frye**)

Everything comes to he who waits – except an Irish bus. (**Maureen Potter**)

It ain't over till the fat lady eats. (**Lenny Bruce**)

A woman's place is in the thong. (**Hugh Hefner**)

A man is known by the company he owns. (**Alan Sugar**)

Philosophy is mind over patter. (**Jonathan King**)

Thou shalt not covet thy neighbour's wife, even though it could be rather cheap to get her home after a date. (**Joseph Carmody**)

You can't make a silk purse if you're not good at that sort of thing. (**Desmond Morrissey**)

Wordsworth sold his birthright for a pot of message. (**Philip Larkin**)

Love means never having to say you're sorry – at least if you're wearing protection. (**Larry Simmonds**)

In space no one can hear you hyperventilate. That's because there's no oxygen. (**Martin Landon**)

Think before you peak. (**Chris Tarrant**)

Opticians' shops are sites for sore eyes. (**Noel V. Ginnity**)

Good pie, missed the chips. (**Frank Muir**)

So little time, so little to do. (**Bob Monkhouse**)

The brain is only as strong as its weakest think. (**Evan Esar**)

Geese should be skein and not herd. (**Robert Morley**)

In politics it rarely pays to be wise before the event. (**Chris Patten**)

Stoichkov is pointing at the bench with his eyes. (**David Pleat**)

The future isn't what it used to be. (**Yogi Berra**)

Paternity is just one bairn thing after another. (**John Williams**)

Winter is the time of year when it gets late early. (**Tony Butler**)

Modern films have to be sin to be appreciated. (**Mary Whitehouse**)

All things come to those who mate. (**Oliver Reed**)

A zebra never changes his spots. (**Dan Quayle**)

The upper crust are just a lot of crumbs sticking together. (**Kenny Everett**)

If all the world's a stage and all the men and women merely players, where does the audience come from? (**Janet Rogers**)

Rugby players are the scrum of the earth. (**Milton Berle**)

Nice guys finish lust. (**Robert Patten**)

The wise man thinks once before he speaks twice. (**Robert Benchley**)

Evil is the root of all money. (**Evan Esar**)

Money isn't everything. It's the only thing. (**Hugh Hefner**)

Dead men tell no solicitors. (**Carl Brahms**)

The want of money is the root of all evil. (**Samuel Butler**)

Show me a good loser and I'll show you a loser. (**Paul Newman**)

A bird in the Strand is worth two in Shepherd's Bush. (**Spike Milligan**)

Anyone for Tennyson? (**Matthew Sturgis**)

Behind every successful man stands a surprised mother-in-law. (**Hubert Humphrey**)

On the other hand, you have five fingers. (**Emo Philips**)

You have to take the sour with the bitter. (**Sam Goldwyn**)

George Porgie, pudding and pie/Kissed the girls and made them cry/When the boys came out to play/He kissed them too/He's funny that way. (**Kenny Everett**)

An oboe is an ill wind that nobody blows good. (**Bennett Cerf**)

Confucius him say: Man who take girl in park have peace on earth. (**Graffiti**)

Bigamy proves that two rites make a wrong. (**Phil Kelly**)

An apple a day keeps the doctor away. An onion a day keeps everyone away. (**Les Dawson**)

An apple a day, if aimed straight, keeps the doctor away. (**P.G. Wodehouse**)

Seek and ye shall find – but usually not what you're looking for. (**George Burns**)

French dockers rule *au quai*. (**Colin Jarman**)

Eat, drink and be merry. Tomorrow the pub is closed. (**Jasper Carrott**)

Eat, drink and be merry: tomorrow we may be radioactive. (**Kenneth Griffith**)

An Irish atheist is a man who wishes to God he could believe in God. (**Dave Allen**)

If this boy keeps his head, the sky's at his feet. (**George Blackburn**)

The immortal Jackie Milburn died today. (**Cliff Morgan**)

Many Hans make Volkswagens work. (**Kenny Everett**)

Today it's politically incorrect to have close encounters with the furred kind. (**Hugh Leonard**)

Roses are reddish, violets are bluish, If it weren't for Hitler, we'd all be Jewish. (**Karl Friedman**)

Laugh and the world laughs with you . But you'll be told to leave the library. (**Janet Rogers**)

Hermaphrodism is an end in itself. (**John Crosbie**)

Uneasy is the head that wears the curlers. (**Bette Midler**)

A verbal contract isn't worth the paper it's written on. (**Sam Goldwyn**)

Love your neighbour but don't get caught. (**Brendan Grace**)

If you can keep your head when all about are losing theirs you probably don't understand the problem. (**Jean Kerr**)

Two can live as cheaply as one ... for half as long. (**Howard Kandel**)

Ready, fire, aim. (**Spike Milligan**)

If you can't stand the heat, stay in the kitchen but move closer to the fridge. (**Bill Cosby**)

Nothing succeeds like failure. (**Oliver Herford**)

Throwing acid is a terrible thing – in some people's eyes. (**Jimmy Carr**)

Will you take this woman to be your awful wedded wife? (**Dylan Thomas**)

Di Matteo's taken to playing in midfield like a duck out of water. (**Peter Osgood**)

He who hesitiates misses the parking spot. (**Tony Hancock**)

Is it kisstomary to cuss the bride? (**William Spooner**)

Make love not war. Or else marry and do both. (**Dave Allen**)

Love thy neighbour - but make sure his wife doesn't find out. (**Tony Hancock**)

There's more than one way to kill a cat which is just as well, as they have nine lives. (**Sidney Faulkner**)

It's tough at the bottom. (**Pete McInerney**)

You go Uruguay and I'll go mine. (**Groucho Marx**)

The proof of the pudding is in the digestion. (**Bill Holland**)

Never let a dago by. Italians are sometimes beautiful. (**Gary Parker**)

Praktiss makes purfikt. (**Victoria Wood**)

Bad spellers of the world untie. (**Kenneth Williams**)

Where there's a pill there's a way. (**Richard Gordon**)

How green was my valet. (**Noel Coward**)

There's always room at the top but you'll probably be very tired after the climb. (**Peter Cook**)

Say it with flowers. Hit him over the head with a bouquet. (**Roseanne**)

Infamy, infamy. Everyone's got it in for me. (**Groucho Marx**)

The wages of sin is birth. (**Derek Walcott**)

Bestiality is a poke in a pig. (**Nigel Rees**)

'Ha ha,' he exclaimed in Portuguese. (**Michael Harkness**)

The way to a man's heart is through his wife's belly. (**Edward Albee**)

The past is history. (**Dave Bassett**)

There comes a time in the affairs of man when he must take the bull by the tail. (**W.C. Fields**)

My favourite actress is Arsula Undress. (**Benny Hill**)

To have an *avant garde* you have to have a *garde*. (**Hugh Casson**)

Don't cry over spilt milk. It could be wine. (**Louis Safian**)

You can lead a horse to water but a pencil must be lead. (**Stan Laurel**)

Man has created God in his image. (**George Santayana**)

King Midas had a gilt complex. (**Terry Adamson**)

Modern plays have to be sin to be appreciated. (**Louis Safian**)

Many are called but few get up. (**Oliver Herford**)

If you want to find your lost youth, cut off his inheritance. (**George Burns**)

He who hesitates is bossed. (**Henny Youngman**)

Actions lie louder than words. (**Carolyn Wells**)

One man's mate is another man's passion. (**Eugene Healy**)

If you give a person a fish they'll fish for a day but if you train a person to fish they'll fish for a lifetime. (**Dan Quayle**)

He hadn't a single redeeming vice. (**Dick Cavett**)

Faith can move mountains. She's a big girl. (**Glenn Hardy**)

Red sky in the morning, sailor take warning. Red sky at night, the barn's on fire. (**Carisa McKeown**)

He who hesitates sometimes wins. (**Lambert Jeffries**)

Man cannot lives by bread alone. He must also have peanut butter. (**James Garfield**)

Julie Andrews is the mother of convention. (**Christopher Plummer**)

It's the Way You Tell 'Em

Holland was saved by being dammed. (**Thomas Hood**)

It ain't over till the fat lady eats. (**John Kammer**)

Kevin Keegan has now tasted the other side of the fence. (**Dave Merrington**)

There but for the grace of God goes God. (**Winston Churchill**)

Man does not live by words alone, despite the fact that he often has to eat them. (**Adlai Stevenson**)

Humpty Dumpty had a great fall - to make up for a bad summer. (**Frank Arnold**)

There was a time when a fool and his money were soon parted. Now it happens to everyone. (**Adlai Stevenson**)

In Turkey I was known as English Delight. (**Noel Coward**)

If it ain't broke don't fix it - unless you're a politician. (**Denis Leary**)

In the spring a young man's fancy turns to things he's been thinking about all winter. (**Hal Roach**)

Money talks. Mine said goodbye. (**Henny Youngman**)

Money doesn't talk, it swears. (**Bob Dylan**)

Do unto others that which you do not wish them to do unto you. (**James Huneker**)

Women. Can't live with them, can't live with them. (**Don Rickles**)

My philosophy of working out is simple: no pain, no pain. (**Carol Liefer**)

Ronald Reagan was a nancyboy. (**Sean Kilroy**)

You're still young if the morning after the night before makes the night before worth the morning after. (**Bob Goddard**)

Time may be a great healer but it's no beauty specialist. (**Herbert Prochnow**)

Mike Tyson suffers from channel vision. (**Frank Bruno**)

Children should be seen and not smelt. (**Carolyn Wells**)

All God's children are not beautiful. Most of God's children, in fact, are barely presentable. (**Fran Lebowitz**)

They say hard work never killed anyone but I figured, why take the chance? (**Ronald Reagan**)

Fools rush in – and usually grab most of the food. (**Joseph Spencer**)

Two can live as cheaply as one - if one doesn't show up. (**Vern McLellan**)

The Lord giveth and the landlord taketh away. (**John Roper**)

Welcome back to the third half. (**Tommy Tiernan**)

A man is judged by the company he keeps solvent. (**Vern McLellan**)

A woman is judged by the company she keeps waiting. (**Hal Roach**)

Let us all live within our means, even if we have to borrow to do so. (**Artemus Ward**)

If you're going to behave like a bastard you better be a genius. (**Jill Craigie**)

The lion will lie down with the lamp but the lamb won't get much sleep. (**Woody Allen**)

Middle age is when work is a lot less fun and fun is a lot more work. (**Milton Berle**)

Any girl who swears she's never been made love to has a right to swear. (**Sophia Loren**)

Age improves with wine. (**George Burns**)

I think there's one smashing rule in life. Never face the facts. (**Barbara Gordon**)

A bird in the hand makes it difficult to blow your nose. (**Richard Betten**)

The way to a man's heart is through his hankie pocket with a bread knife. (**Jo Brand**)

Life is too short to stuff a mushroom. (**Shirley Conran**)

Turning the other cheek is a kind of moral ju-jitsu. (**Stanley Lee**)

Laziness is the mother of intention. (**Agatha Christie**)

The hand that rocked the cradle kicked the bucket. (**Sam Goldwyn**)

Ashes to ashes, clay to clay. If the enemy don't get you, your own folks may. (**James Thurber**)

Stick and stones may break my bones but names will break our hearts. (**Robert Fulghum**)

Jesus saves, but Lionel Messi knocks them in from the rebounds. (**Gary Lineker**)

The road to hell is paved with good conventions. (**Louis Berman**)

Immigration is the sincerest form of flattery. (**Jack Paar**)

When things just can't get any worse, they will. (**Arthur Bloch**)

History doesn't repeat itself. Historians repeat one another. (**Jonathan Miller**)

No matter where you go, there you are. (**Tony Butler**)

Space is almost infinite. (**Dan Quayle**)

Although God can't alter the past, historians can. (**Samuel Butler**)

If you want to pull the wool over your wife's eyes you need a good yarn. (**Gyles Brandreth**)

People who swim in Dublin these days are just going through the motions. (**Brendan Behan**)

Out of the mouths of babes - and usually when you've got your best clothes on. (**Erma Bombeck**)

If the shoe fits, ask for another pair to put by for when it wears out. (**Tony Hancock**)

Never eat on an empty stomach. (**Dawn French**)

In the midst of life we are in debt. (**Ethel Watts Mumford**)

Never change diapers in midstream. (**Don Marquis**)

Ask not for whom the bell tolls. Let the answering machine get it. (**Jean Kerr**)

I like to wake up every morning feeling a new man. (**Jean Harlow**)

Televangelists are ecumenical with the truth. (**John Crosbie**)

The only thing that experience teaches us is that experience teaches us nothing. (**Andre Maurois**)

Cosmetic surgeons give the bust that money can buy. (**Jackie Collins**)

The darkest hour is just before you turn the lights on. (**Bert Hanley**)

Boys will be boys, and so will a lot of middle-aged men. (**Kin Hubbard**)

Every crowd has a silver lining. (**Phineas T. Barnum**)

The Sydney Opera House is off Quay. (**Clive James**)

Any stigma will do to beat a dogma. (**Philip Guedalla**)

Truth is duller than fiction. (**Piers Paul Reid**)

Give the devil his pew. (**Malcolm Muggeridge**)

Always speak your mind, whether you mean it or not.
(**Rodney Dangerfield**)

My second hit was a flop. (**Shakin' Stevens**)

Give a woman an inch and she'll park a car on it. (**E.B. White**)

Only quadrupeds should talk about putting their best foot forward. Human just have better ones. (**Lambert Jeffries**)

What you don't know can't hurt you unless it's a JCB coming up on your blind side. (**Joseph Carroll**)

It takes two to tango but you can do a lot of the more modern dances on your own. (**Herbert Spencer**)

Give a man enough rope and he won't ask you for any more.
(**Will Rogers**)

Smoking damages your cigarettes. (**David Niven**)

Oliver Hardy rested on his laurel. (**Barry Norman**)

A curved line is the loveliest distance between two points.
(**Mae West**)

The dullest hour is before the yawn. (**Harry Secombe**)

Aardvark never killed anyone. (**Spike Milligan**)

All power corrupts, and horsepower corrupts absolutely. (**John Hillaby**)

All work and no play makes Jack's wife a rich widow. (**Tom McDermott**)

Smoking is a dying habit. (**Virginia Bottomley**)

My life is so full of surprises, nothing surprises me any more. (**Kim Wilde**)

Children are great comforters in old age but they may not allow you to reach it. (**Lionel Kauffman**)

Work is the curse of the drinking classes. (**Oscar Wilde**)

Work is the curse of the working classes. (**Brendan Behan**)

Many false words are spoken in jest. (**Kenneth Tynan**)

Power corrupts, but lack of power corrupts absolutely. (**Adlai Stevenson**)

Ask not what you can do for your country. Ask what's for lunch. (**Orson Welles**)

Ask not what you can do for your country for they're liable to tell you. (**Mark Steinbeck**)

The meek shall inherit the earth if that's all right with the rest of you. (**Kevin Sampson**)

If the meek shall inherit the earth it's only because they wouldn't have the nerve to refuse it. (**Jackie Vernon**)

I wonder what would have happened if the shirt had been on the other foot. (**Mike Walker**)

The future will be better tomorrow. (**Dan Quayle**)

One man's feet are another man's poison. (**Richard Cussons**)

I get on with everyone except people. (**Charles Bukowski**)

Age shall not wither her, nor iron bars a cage. (**Kenneth Wlliams**)

A woman can't be too rich, too thin, or have too many silk blouses. (**Joyce Jillson**)

Royal reporters are *la crème de la scum*. (**Harry Arnold**)

There'll never be another ewe – even with sheep cloning. (**Don Griffith**)

Mothers feed the hand that bites them. (**Peter de Vries**)

Love flies out the door when money comes innuendo. (**S.J. Perelman**)

This boy has been burning the midnight oil at both ends. (**Sid Waddell**)

If it's not baroque, don't fix it. (**Linda Wolverton**)

Stay with me. I want to be alone. (**Joey Adams**)

Only the young die good. (**Oliver Herford**)

Being busy is the best excuse for not working. (**Kenneth Tynan**)

Punctuality is the virtue of the bored. (**Des Bishop**)

A secret may sometimes be best kept by keeping the secret of it being a secret. (**Sir Henry Taylor**)

One good turn and you have most of the bed covers. (**Elaine Moore**)

Have they ever found a link between asbestos and asbestos-related diseases? (**Jimmy Young**)

Abstinence is the thin end of the pledge. (**Arnold Miller**)

A shotgun wedding is a matter of wife or death. (**Peter Cagney**)

Women usually like men with a will of their own – made out in their favour. (**Brendan Behan**)

Because of inflation, it now takes a loaf and a half to be better than no bread. (**Dave Wilder**)

Don't trust your first impulses - they're always good. (**Talleyrand**)

More waist, less speed. (**David Walters**)

Charity begins at homelessness. (**Jay Cocks**)

A fat wife is a bird in a girdled cage. (**Jerry Lewis**)

If you want to dress to please your husband, wear last year's clothes. (**Joey Bishop**)

War hath no fury like a non-combatant. (**C.E. Montague**)

Old cooks never die. They just go to pot. (**James Oliver**)

Variety is the spice of wife. (**Gene Perret**)

Posh Spice is the variety of life. (**David Beckham**)

Invention is the mother of necessity. (**Thorstein Veblen**)

If we start counting our chickens before they hatch they won't lay any eggs in the basket. (**Bobby Robson**)

An apology is the only thing that will enable you to have the last word with a woman. (**Peter Cagney**)

Cleanliness is only next to godliness in an Irish dictionary. (**Malcolm Bennett**)

Cleanliness is next to impossible. (**Fran Lebowitz**)

Better latent than never. (**Graham Norton**)

Laugh and the world laughs with you. Weep and it laughs even more. (**Eric Idle**)

Generally Speaking

A rose by any other name would be just as expensive. (**Spike Milligan**)

Everything in our favour was against us. (**Danny Blanchflower**)

Two wrongs may not make a right but they make a hell of a good excuse. (**Thomas Szasz**)

I have a lisp. I like to call a spade a thpade. (**Oliver Herford**)

Since we have to speak well of the dead, let's knock 'em while they're alive. (**John Sloan**)

George Bush was born with a silver foot in his mouth. (**Ann Richard**)

There's no place like Rome. (**John Huston**)

Warren Beatty used to treat all men like sequels. (**Joan Collins**)

It was a no-win situation so I'm glad I won. (**Frank Bruno**)

You live and learn - and then you die and forget it all. (**Noel Coward**)

It takes a lot of experience for a girl to kiss like a beginner. (**Mae West**)

Reality is a crutch for people who can't cope with drugs. (**Lily Tomlin**)

God is love - but get it in writing. (**Gypsy Rose Lee**)

Once you're dead you're made for life. (**Jimi Hendrix**)

Smart secretaries never miss a period. (**Bob Hope**)

Cannibals love their neighbours - with sauce. (**Jean Rigaux**)

I think, therefore I am - I think. (**Howard Schneider**)

Two's company; three's accrued. (**Peter Cagney**)

The early bird usually wishes he'd let someone else get up first. (**Elliot Gould**)

Candy is dandy but liquor is quicker. (**Ogden Nash**)

Once a king always a king but once a night's enough. (**Brian Johnston**)

Don't just do something, stand there. (**Clint Eastwood**)

We're all cremated equal. (**Goodman Ace**)

Happiness can't buy money. (**Spike Milligan**)

The days of the digital watch are numbered. (**Dave Arnold**)

Never judge a book by the motion picture. (**William Goldman**)

Yorick was a numbskull. (**Kevin Hayes**)

Donald Duck isn't all he's quacked up to be. (**Pam Ayres**)

Jesus saves. And at today's prices that's a real miracle. (**Josh Bradley**)

A thing of beauty costs a small fortune. (**Jilly Cooper**)

A pun is the lowest form of wit – unless you thought of it first. (**George Gobel**)

The best track on that album isn't on it. (**Jimmy Young**)

Thank God I'm an atheist. (**Luis Bunuel**)

Cricket shouldn't be used as a political football. (**David Graveney**)

Accidents will happen in the best regulated families though they're less frequent now with birth control. (**Noel Creswell**)

TB or not TB, that is congestion. (**Woody Allen**)

Beware of Greeks bearing gifts. Especially if they're on Special. (**Bob Monkhouse**)

If it wasn't for Venetian blinds it would be curtains for all of us. (**Kenny Everett**)

I've been burning the midday oil. (**Ronald Reagan**)

The reason we lost is because we didn't win. (**Cristiano Ronaldo**)

The best-laid plans of mice and men end up on the cutting room floor. (**P.G. Wodehouse**)

Absence makes the heart go wander. (**Kenneth Williams**)

Colonic irrigation isn't to be sniffed at. (**Jennifer Saunders**)

Gertrude Stein was the mama of dada. (**Andy Warhol**)

Einstein Rules Relatively OK. (**George Wilton**)

The silence is getting louder. (**Dave Woods**)

Hell hath no fury like vested interest masquerading as moral principle. (**Evelyn Waugh**)

In spite of the cost of living it's still very popular. (**George Burns**)

The greatest undeveloped territories in the world are between people's ears. (**Samuel Herbert**)

Reincarnation is making a comeback. (**George Coote**)

To thine own self be false. Who else will know? (**Denis Goodwin**)

Don't become a clairvoyant: there's no future in it. (**Jackie Mason**)

TV can be very educational if it drives you out of the living-room into the library. (**Groucho Marx**)

To know Barbra Streisand isn't necessarily to love her. (**Rex Reed**)

Better to have loved a short man than never to have loved a tall. (**Miles Kington**)

He looked like a cat on a hot brick roof. (**John Francome**)

Uneasy is the head that faces the guillotine. (**Paula Greene**)

A friend in need is a bloody nuisance. (**Colin Crompton**)

Age cannot with her, nor custom stale her infinite virginity. (**Daniel Webster**)

It took a lot of bottle for Tony Adams to admit he was an alcoholic. (**Ian Wright**)

I don't see the point of hiding a bushel under a carpet. (**Mel B**)

Just because you're paranoid doesn't mean they're not out to get you. (**Henry Kissinger**)

Life doesn't imitate art. It imitates bad television. (**Woody Allen**)

Tottenham haven't thrown in the towel even though they've been under the gun. (**Bobby Charlton**)

One swallow doesn't make a slummer. (**Kenneth Tynan**)

I've developed a new philosophy: I now only dread one day at a time. (**Charles Schulz**)

Technology owes ecology an apology. (**Alan Eddison**)

Some things have to be believed to be seen. (**Ralph Hodgson**)

It's an ill wind that blows when you leave the hairdresser. (**Phyllis Diller**)

Bachelors believe in the happiness of pursuit. (**Helen Rowland**)

After the ceasefire in Northern Ireland, tourism went shooting up. (**Jim Wallace**)

All work and no play makes Jack a very tired boy. (**John Day**)

Procrastination is the art of keeping up with yesterday. (**Osbert Sitwell**)

Bob Hope springs infernal. (**Sam Kunison**)

A woman is a thing of beauty and an expense forever. (**Leopold Fechtner**)

If you think before you speak, the other fellow gets in his joke first. (**Ed Howe**)

People who jump to conclusions rarely alight on them. (**Philip Guadella**)

Winning isn't everything. It's the only thing. (**Vince Lombardi**)

Platini was given a great reception after he went off. (**Elton Welsby**)

It's dog eat dog in this rat race. (**John Deacon**)

A wise woman will always let her husband have her way. (**R.B. Sheridan**)

Time is a great teacher but unfortunately it kills all its pupils. (**Hector Berlioz**)

Laugh and the world laughs with you. Snore and you sleep alone. (**Beatrice Campbell**)

We've already hunted the grey whale into extinction twice. (**Andrea Arnold**)

There's no safety in numbers - or in anything else either. (**James Thurber**)

A watched kettle never boils, especially if you didn't pay your ESB bill. (**Maureen Potter**)

Brides goeth before a fall. (**Russell Brown**)

Trust in God - she will provide. (**Emmeline Pankhurst**)

There's no such thing as a small whiskey. (**Oliver St. John Gogarty**)

Familiarity breeds contempt but you can't breed without familiarity. (**Maxim Navolik**)

Familiarity breeds contempt - and children. (**Mark Twain**)

A comedian who repeats old gags is a clear case of the tale dogging the wag. (**Louis Safian**)

The opera ain't over till the fat lady blocks the Exit. (**Peter Boyle**)

He chanced his arm with his left foot. (**Trevor Brooking**)

If you don't get what you like in life, you better learn to like what you get. (**G.K. Chesterton**)

A man cannot be too careful in his choice of enemies. (**Oscar Wilde**)

Blessed is he who expects nothing for he shall never be disappointed. (**Alexander Pope**)

Save the gerund. Screw the whale. (**Tom Stoppard**)

Necessity is the smotherer of convention. (**Lambert Jeffries**)

Gandhi wasn't the man that his mother was the woman. (**Eldon Griffiths**)

Don't call your child Arthur. These days every Tom, Dick and Harry is called Arthur. (**Samuel Goldwyn**)

The earth shall inherit the meek. (**Goodman Ace**)

One disadvantage of being a hog is that some fool might try to make a silk purse out of your wife's ear. (**J.B. Morton**)

If an experiment works, something has gone wrong. (**Evelyn Waugh**)

The customer is always right except at the beginning of an assertiveness course. (**Jean Kerr**)

Pornography offers a vice to the lovelorn. (**Gregory Skinner**)

Sado-masochism means never having to say you're sorry. (**Sam Kushner**)

To appreciate newspapers you have to read between the lies. (**Goodman Ace**)

An open marriage is nature's way of telling you you need a divorce. (**Bob Monkhouse**)

Some men are born mediocre, some achieve mediocrity and some have mediocrity thrust upon them. (**Joseph Heller**)

Suffer fools gladly; they may be right. (**Holbrook Jackson**)

Working mothers are the backbone of the third half of the economy. (**Glenda Jackson**)

You're only as old as you field. (**Babe Ruth**)

You're only as old as the woman you're feeling. (**Groucho Marx**)

Eskimos are God's frozen people. (**Ronnie Corbett**)

Muhammad Ali Rules KO. (**Michael Parkinson**)

In God we trust. All others must pay. (**Sign over bar counter**)

I was feeling as sick as the proverbial donkey. (**Mick McCarthy**)

All men are born equal but some of them get married. (**Phil Silvers**)

You don't have to fool all the people all the time – just enough to get elected. (**Gerald Barzan**)

Home wasn't built in a day. (**Jane Ace**)

America is the land of permanent waves and impermanent wives. (**Brendan Behan**)

Veni vidi, VD. (**Julie Birchill**)

They are not long, the days of whine and poses. (**Jasper Carrott**)

History is a record of events that didn't happen written by somebody who wasn't there. (**Jasper Carrott**)

Things You Should Know

Out of the mouths of babes comes food. (**Les Dawson**)

Dying can damage your health. Every coffin should contain a Government Health Warning. (**Spike Milligan**)

Manslaughter is a terrible thing. Woman's laughter is even worse. (**Henny Youngman**)

Look, hesitate, leap. (**Michael Caine**)

Roses are red, violets are blue. In fact everyone is wearing multi-coloured knickers these days. (**Gary Midlock**)

The trouble with mixing business and pleasure is that pleasure usually gets priority. (**Dave Allen**)

I may have my faults but being wrong ain't one of them. (**Jimmy Hoffa**)

The cup of Ireland's miseries has been overflowing for centuries and is not yet half full. (**Sir Boyle Roche**)

More hash, less speed. (**Keith Richard**)

A fool and his money get invited to all the best parties. (**Andy Warhol**)

Television is now so hungry for material they're scraping the *top* of the barrel. (**Gore Vidal**)

Feminists should be put behind bras. (**Norman Mailer**)

All that glitters isn't Gary. (**Cliff Wilson**)

There's no time like the present for postponing what you don't want to do. (**Quentin Crisp**)

What you don't owe can't hurt you. (**Jack Benny**)

Equality of opportunity means equal opportunity to be unequal. (**Iain MacLeod**)

Parking is such street sorrow. (**Herb Caen**)

Obesity is a *fat accompli*. (**Len Elliott**)

The only good Tory is a lavatory. (**Russell Brand**)

There's nothing wrong with sobriety in moderation. (**John Ciardi**)

I understand the importance of bondage between parent and child. (**Dan Quayle**)

Mary had a little lamb. That'll teach her to stay out of the barn. (**Blanche Knott**)

Never put off till tomorrow what you can do the day after. (**Hal Roach**)

First things first. Second things never. (**Shirley Conran**)

Actors believe he who's without fault should stone the cast first. (**John Gielgud**)

Neil Diamond is a girl's best friend. (**Barbra Streisand**)

A fool and his money are soon partied. (**Bob Hope**)

Anything worth doing is worth doing badly. (**G.K. Chesterton**)

Good news is no news. (**Lambert Jeffries**)

Ignorance is bliss, despite the fact that a lot of politicians look happy. (**Lily Tomlin**)

Bobby Robson must be thinking of throwing some fresh legs on. **(Kevin Keegan)**

The typewriter, ½ike all mac&hines, has amind of it sown. **(A.B. Herbert)**

Once he'd gone past the point of no return there was no going back. **(Murray Hill)**

A chrysanthemum by any other name would he much easier to spell. **(William Johnston)**

What you get free costs too much. **(Jean Anouilh)**

Macho doesn't prove mucho. **(Zsa Zsa Gabor)**

To err is humour. **(Bob Monkhouse)**

Avoid drugs. The only dope worth shooting is Donald Trump **(Michael Moore)**

The population explosion was caused by overbearing women. **(Frank Carson)**

As ye smoke, so shall ye reek. **(Heather Johnston)**

If you can't say anything good about a person, sit right here by me. (**Alice Roosevelt Longworth**)

Ann Bancroft was an undergraduate. (**Dustin Hoffman**)

Don't just stand there - undo something. (**Bob Hope**)

Strike while the shop steward is on your side. (**Harry Wilson**)

A woman is never too old to yearn. (**Addison Mizner**)

When in Rome, do as the Greeks. (**Denis Donoghue**)

If I can't take it with me I'm not going. (**Jack Benny**)

Many are cold but few are frozen. (**Frank Muir**)

Every journalist has a novel in him, which is an excellent place for it. (**Russell Lyons**)

Every silver lining has a cloud attached to it. (**Sheila Levinson**)

Greta Garbo always took the elevator to avoid the stares. (**Billy Wilder**)

If something goes without saying, let it. (**Jacob Braude**)

Inside every fat man there's a thin man trying to get out and outside every thin woman there's a fat man trying to get in. (**Katherine Whitehorse**)

The only way to prevent what's past is to put a stop to it before it happens. (**Sir Boyle Roche**)

If at first you don't succeed, blame the wife. (**Tommy Cooper**)

Just when you think you can make both ends meet, somebody moves the ends. (**Pansy Penner**)

An alcoholic is someone who drinks more than you do. (**Dylan Thomas**)

The thing about a politician is, you have to take the smooth with the smooth. (**Susan Hill**)

It's easy for a girl to stay on the straight and narrow if she's built that way. (**Zsa Zsa Gabor**)

In heaven an angel is nobody in particular. (**George Bernard Shaw**)

When you're down and out something always turns up. But it's usually the noses of your friends. (**Orson Welles**)

A Rolling Stone gathers Kate Moss. (**David Sindon**)

Familiarity doesn't breed contempt. It breeds more familiarity. (**Gertrude Stein**)

They stayed away in droves. (**Sam Goldwyn**)

Divorces are made in heaven. (**Oscar Wilde**)

The phrase 'Home Sweet Home' must have been written by a bachelor. (**Samuel Butler**)

Man proposes – but not always marriage. (**Graham Norton**)

Marriage is bed and bored. (**George Sanders**)

Capitalism exploits man. With communism it's the other way round. (**Geoffrey Green**)

Think twice before you speak and you'll find everyone talking about something else. (**Francis Rodman**)

Grammar books are parse for the course. (**John Crosbie**)

A nickel ain't worth a dime anymore. (**Yogi Berra**)

You must put your foot down with a firm hand. ((**Michael Van Stratten**)

Hope is the feeling that the feeling you have isn't permanent. (**Jean Kerr**)

Money can't buy happiness. That's why we have credit cards. (**Red Skelton**)

You need someone to love you while you're looking for someone to love. (**Shelagh Delaney**)

To err is human, to forgive unusual. (**Bill Maher**)

To err is human. To really foul things up requires a computer. (**Philip Howard**)

Amor vincit insomnia. (**Christopher Fry**)

There's no fool like an oiled fool. (**Leopold Fechtner**)

When poverty comes in the door, the cheque book flies out the window. (**Jack Benny**)

Vasectomy means never having to say you're sorry. (**Larry Adler**)

This show is an end of season curtain raiser. (**Peter White**)

Statistics will prove anything, even the truth. (**Mark Twain**)

The only certainties in life are death, taxes, and supermarket trollies with wobbly legs. (**Victoria Wood**)

None but the brave deserve affairs. (**Don Rickles**)

Psychology is the art of producing habits from rats. (**Frank Carson**)

Sorrow is tranquillity remembered in emotion. (**Dorothy Parker**)

Irish dancing requires a stiff upper hip. (**John Crosbie**)

Every dog has his day but only those with broken tails have weak ends. (**Janet Rogers**)

Where there's life there's tax. (**Gay Byrne**)

Gynaecologists - look up a friend today. (**Bruce Ridley**)

Better to have loved and lost than to have to buy shoes for eight kids. (**William Walton**)

Better to have loved and lost, but only if you have a good lawyer. (**Herb Caen**)

When everybody is somebody, nobody is anybody. (**Hilaire Belloc**)

Only the hot dog feeds the hand that bits it. (**Peter Cagney**)

Many a true word is spoken undressed. (**H.L. Mencken**)

Sex is when the loin lies down with the limb. (**Conrad Aiken**)

Don't count your chickens before they cross the road. (**Steven Wright**)

Once bitten, twice injected. (**Leonard Rossiter**)

Home is where the DVD is. (**Joe Templar**)

Oh what a tangled web we weave, when first we practise to conceive. (**Don Herold**)

There's less to life than meets the eye. (**Woody Allen**)

At my age travel broadens the behind. (**Stephen Fry**)

In spring a young man's fancy turns to things he's been thinking about all winter. (**Hal Roach**)

Gigolos live by the sweat of their fraus. (**Chris Furlong**)

Impropriety is the soul of wit. (**W. Somerset Maugham**)

Mozart was an opera-tunist. (**John Crosbie**)

The champion has just retired after eight undefeated victories. (**Richard Whiteley**)

Loneliness is a bastard on Father's Day. (**Kenny Everett**)

Anyone who says he sleeps like a baby obviously hasn't got one. (**James Simpson**)

Money can't buy you friends; just a better class of enemy. (**Spike Milligan**)

I saw Marilyn Monroe last week. Her bottom has gone to pot and her pot has gone to bottom. (**Kenneth Tynan**)

One good turn gets most of the duvet. (**Victoria Wood**)

Jerusalem wasn't built in a day. (**Robert Maxwell**)

Puritans 'no' what they like. (**Leopold Fechtner**)

Archaeology proves you can't keep a good man down. (**Agatha Christie**)

Truths Universally Acknowleged

Audio-typists take too much for grunted. (**Herbert Prochnow**)

If you can't remember whether you ever had amnesia you probably did. (**Gerald Crowley**)

Meditation beats sitting around all day doing nothing. (**Eric Idle**)

I made some yes men an offer last week. They said no. (**Billy Wilder**)

Women are the stronger sex because of the weakness of the stronger sex for the weaker sex. (**Graham Buckley**)

This will be remembered as a season best forgotten. (**Terry Badoo**)

A bird in the hand is probably going to give you salmonella. (**Roy Brown**)

A bird in the hand is useless if you want to pick your nose. (**Quentin Crisp**)

Gay's okay but hetero was bettero. (**Michael Sheridan**)

Apathy Rules O. (**Denis Leary**)

Circumcision is a rip-off. (**Gary Manson**)

Yea though I walk in the valley of the death I shall fear no evil - because I'm the meanest SOB in it. (**George Carlin**)

As far as bees are concerned there's no place like comb. (**Peter Bowles**)

There's no time like the present for postponing what we don't want to do. (**Joe Daly**)

Nothing ventured nothing lost. (**Jennifer Wright**)

Red sky in the morning, red wine last night. (**Pam Ayres**)

A fool and his money are soon parted. What I want to know is how they got together in the first place. (**Cyril Fletcher**)

Jack and Jill went up the hill. Now Jill's father is having a chat with Jack about something. (**Dan Porter**)

Amnesia Rules O. (**Nigel Rees**)

Mary had a little lamb. The gynaecologists are looking into it. (**Denis Skinner**)

If you're married, it only takes one to quarrel. (**Ogden Nash**)

A leotard can never change its spots. (**Liza Minnelli**)

Behind every successful man stands an amazed woman. (**Helen Rowland**)

Whiskey makes you see double and feel single. (**Frank Hall**)

The best things in life are tax deductible. (**Les Dawson**)

I'll give you a definite maybe. (**Sam Goldwyn**)

God never shuts one door but He closes another. (**Ardal O'Hanlon**)

Are Chinese voyeurs known as Peking Toms? (**Les Dawson**)

The bigger they are, the harder they maul. (**Howard Kandel**)

Beauty is only sin deep. (**George Sanders**)

Beauty is only skin deep. Ugly goes to the bone. (**Phyllis Diller**)

If all the people who slept through after-dinner speeches were laid end to end…. they'd be a lot more comfortable. (**Herbert Prochnow**)

Sailors like a port in every wife. (**Brian Johnston**)

Black is beautiful - but unemployed. (**Bill Cosby**)

America has a funny attitude to celebrity. O.J. Simpson walked and Christopher Reeve got the electric chair. (**Jay Leno**)

To itch is human, to scratch divine. (**Bette Midler**)

Brevity is the soul of lingerie. (**Dorothy Parker**)

The course of true love never runs smooth. In the worst case scenarios, it leads to marriage. (**Andy Kaufman**)

Money can't buy happiness, just a more pleasant form of misery. (**Anthony Butler**)

Marriage is grand. Divorce is twenty grand. (**Chevy Chase**)

Most of my clichés aren't original. (**Chuck Knox**)

Two wongs don't make a white. (**Arthur Calwell**)

Money is better than poverty if only for financial reasons. (**Woody Allen**)

Two beds are better than one. (**Warren Beatty**)

I wish I was what I used to be when I wished I was what I am. (**Therese Cafferky**)

Love is blind but your mother-in-law isn't. (**Evan Esar**)

Love is blind. Marriage is a tin opener. (**Fred Allen**)

Old age is when actions creak louder than words. (**Bob Hope**)

There are none so blind as those who are on their way to the optician. (**Bob Monkhouse**)

Hell hath no fury like a woman's corns. (**Leonard Levinson**)

Marry in haste; repeat at leisure. (**James Cabell**)

The hand that rocks the cradle is usually attached to someone who isn't getting enough sleep. (**Jim Fiebig**)

When your boat finally does come in, it's often the Titanic. (**Trevor Griffiths**)

Parking is such street sorrow. (**Herb Caen**)

Too many cooks spoil the figure. (**Phyllis Diller**)

What shall it profit a man if he gains the whole world and then there's a recession? (**Mel Brooks**)

His bark is worse than his bite if he's been eating garlic. (**Red Skelton**)

Plastic surgeons make mountains out of molehills. (**Dolly Parton**)

Beauty is in the eye of the beholder. Get it out with Optrex. (**Spike Milligan**)

Perhaps the straight and narrow path would be wider if more people used it. (**Kay Ingram**)

Only the insane take themselves really seriously. (**Max Beerbohm**)

To me, Adler will always be Jung. (**Max Wall**)

Two is company. Three's allowed. (**Fred Allen**)

Those whom the gods would destroy they first put working for MTV. (**Don Buckley**)

A bit of talcum is always walcum. (**Ogden Nash**)

If you don't know where you're going you'll wind up somewhere else. (**Yogi Berra**)

Grime doesn't pay. (**John Crosbie**)

Treat others as you would have them treat you. Unless, of course, you're a masochist. (**Bob Monkhouse**)

You *can* have your cake and eat it, but you'll get fat as a result, (**Julian Barnes**)

A verbal contract isn't worth the paper it's written on. (**Sam Goldwyn**)

Egyptologists are Mummy's boys. (**Sean Kilroy**)

Don't burn your bridges while you're changing horses in midstream, (**Stanley Walker**)

Don't cross your bridges till you burn them. (**Dick Bower**)

Don't change houses in mid-dream. (**John Farman**)

Behind every successful man is a fish with a bicycle. (**Gloria Steinem**)

Braggarts enter conversations feat first. (**Louis Safian**)

A guilty conscience is the mother of invention. (**Carolyn Wells**)

Look before you bite. (**Grant Loomis**)

Don't judge a book by its lover. (**Kenneth Tynan**)

A bookmaker is a wizard of odds. (**Peter Cagney**)

He who laughs last is probably trying to think of a *double entendre*. (**Gary Cussins**)

Diplomacy is the art of letting someone else have your way. (**Daniele Very**)

If you covered a sow's ear with silk purses, the bristles would still work their way through. (**Marie Lloyd**)

A fool and his money are soon popular. (**Fred Metcalf**)

Here today and, as far as the neighbours are concerned, here tomorrow as well. (**Peg Bracken**)

Anything said off the cuff has usually been written on it first. (**Robin Skelton**)

When I'm good I'm very very good and when I'm bad I'm even better. (**Mae West**)

Television is the bland leading the bland. (**Johnny Carson**)

There will come a day when the atom splits the man. (**Peter Cagney**)

If music be the food of love let's have a Beethoven butty. (**John Lennon**)

Youth is stranger than fiction. (**Dorothy Fuldheim**)

Once upon a time there was no time. (**John Barrow**)

Variety is the life of spies. (**Ian Fleming**)

One man's fish is another man's *poisson*. (**Carolyn Wells**)

Thirst come, thirst served. (**W.C. Fields**)

To pee or no to pee, that is the question. (**Jane Darrow**)

Greater love than this no man hath than that he lay down his friends for his life. (**JeremyThorpe**)

Publish and be sued. (**Richard Ingrams**)

To eat is human, to digest divine. (**CharlesCopeland**)

Every man should have a wife - preferably his own. (**Zsa Zsa Gabor**)

The wages of sin is alimony. (**Carolyn Wells**)

I climbed the ladder of success wrong by wrong. (**Mae West**)

We can forgive those who bore us. We can never forgive those whom we bore. (**Duc De La Rochefoucauld**)

A friend that isn't in need is a friend indeed. (**Kin Hubbard**)

A friend with weed is a friend indeed. (**Kinky Friedman**)

I'm a wonderful housekeeper. Every time I get divorced I keep the house. (**Zsa Zsa Gabor**)

When you've seen one nuclear war you've seen them all. (**Billy Connolly**)

The family that preys together stays together. (**Mario Puzo**)

Beauty is in the eye of the beerholder. (**Jim Davison**)

They also serve who only punctuate. (**Brian Moore**)

Contempt breeds familiarity. (**Kenneth Tynan**)

Hell hath no fury like a hustler with a literary agent. (**Frank Sinatra**)

Nothing is more real than nothing. (**Samuel Beckett**)

The meek won't inherit the earth unless they're prepared to fight for their meekness. (**Harold Lasker**)

The chief knowledge we get from books is that very few of them are worth reading. (**Cyril Connolly**)

If money doesn't grow on trees, how come banks have so many branches? (**Fred Metcalf**)

I used to think monogamy was a kind of furniture. (**Warren Beatty**)

Oedipus was a nervous rex. (**Jonathan Miller**)

Misery loves company but it can't bear competition. (**Josh Billings**)

A penny saved is a pocket burned. (**Louis Copeland**)

Women were God's second mistake. (**Friedrich Nietzsche**)

Nostalgia ain't what it used to be. (**Simone Signoret**)

Man does not live by GNP alone. (**Paul Samuelson**)

Some are born lazy, some have laziness thrust upon them and others spend a great deal of effort creating a careless nonchalance. (**Beryl Downing**)

It takes two to tangle. (**Johnny Carson**)

Absinthe makes the tart grow fonder. (**Hugh Drummond**)

A word to the wise is unnecessary. It's the idiots who need it. (**Sam Fuller**)

Always speak ill of the dead. They can't sue. (**Lee Marvin**)

Spare the rod and spoil the fish. (**Jack Charlton**)

Nothing succeeds like reputation. (**John Huston**)

An unwatched pot boils immediately. (**H.F. Ellis**)

Mary had a little lamb - the midwife fainted. (**Leonard Rossiter**)

Are We Missing Something Here?

When a man tells me he's going to put all his cards on the table I always look up his sleeve. (**Leslie Belisha**)

Gambling is a sure way of getting nothing for something. (**Wilson Mizner**)

Some girls shrink from sex but others get bigger and bigger. (**SteveMartin**)

Perhaps it was because Nero fiddled that they burned Rome. (**Oliver Herford**)

Money may be the root of all evil but people need roots. (**Joel Rothman**)

Winsome, lose some. (**Alan Bennett**)

You only live once but the way I live, that's enough. (**Frank Sinatra**)

Norman Mailer is the master of the *single entendre*. (**Gore Vidal**)

The family that rakes together aches together. (**Lionel Jackson**)

Travel doesn't broaden the mind. It just lengthens the conversation. (**Elizabeth Drew**)

A watched pot never boils but if you look the other way there'll be a terrible mess of your cooker. (**Edward Stevenson**)

One swallow doesn't make a summer but it can sure break a New Year resolution. (**Sally Jesse Raphael**)

Jesus loves you. Everyone else knows you're an asshole. (**Bill Hicks**)

Life is one damn thing after another. (**Elbert Hubbard**)

Life is one damn thing over and over again. (**Edna St. Vincent Millay**)

Blessed are the young. They shall inherit the National Debt. (**Herbert Hoover**)

A burden in the bush is worth two in the hand. (**James Thurber**)

Immortality is a fate worse than death. (**Edgar Shoaff**)

One swallow doesn't make a pint. (**Brendan Behan**)

The email of the species is deadlier than the male. (**Stephen Fry**)

A hair in the hand is worth two in the brush. (**Declan Crowley**)

Coin collectors only get together for old dimes sake. (**John Crosbie**)

I improve on misquotation. (**Cary Grant**)

A kiss that speaks volumes is rarely a first edition. (**Claire Whiting**)

Timidity rules if that's okay with the rest of you. (**Nigel Rees**)

Yoga is the be-all and bend-all. (**John Crosbie**)

Verlaine is always chasing Rimbauds. (**Dorothy Parker**)

You can't think rationally on an empty stomach. And not many people can do so on a full one either. (**Lord Reith**)

Good taste is better than bad taste but bad taste is better than no taste. (**Bertolt Brecht**)

I'm footloose and fiancée-free. (**George Best**)

As ye sew, so shall ye rip. (**Heather McKenzie**)

Scratch a lover and find a foe. (**Dorothy Parker**)

Self-love seems so often unrequited. (**Anthony Powell**)

There's no place like home - after the pubs close. (**Brendan Behan**)

Pornography is in the groin of the beholder. (**Charles Rember**)

Marriage is only for a little while. It's alimony that lasts forever. (**Quentin Crisp**)

Sleep is an excellent way of listening to an opera. (**James Stephens**)

Love is a temporary insanity curable by marriage. (**Ambrose Bierce**)

Incompatibility is the spice of love - provided he has the income and she's pattable. (**Ogden Nash**)

The world is my lobster. (**Leon Griffiths**)

Actresses will happen in the best-regulated families. (**Oliver Herford**)

Showbusiness isn't just dog eat dog. It's dog won't return dog's phone calls. (**Woody Allen**)

The family that prays together stays together. Thank God my father left home. (**Les Dawson**)

If you're not fired with enthusiasm you'll be fired with enthusiasm. (**Paul Getty**)

Omnia vincit amor. (**Dave Allen**)

Divorce is the future tense of marriage. (**John Barrymore**)

If you're wandering lonely as a cloud you're probably anti-social. (**Eric Idle**)

Don't hit a man while he's down. He might get up and hit you back. (**Big O**)

In the land of the blind, one-eyed men keep bumping into trees. (**Jackie Mason**)

Two can starve as cheaply as one. (**Herbert Prochnow**)

There's no time like the pleasant. (**Nigel Rees**)

He who hesitates has just read the small print. (**P.J. O'Rourke**)

Sticks and stones may break my bones but names will never hurt me because I'll sue you for slander. (**George Sanders**)

Women who think the way to a man's heart is through is stomach are aiming a bit too high. (**Julie Birchill**)

Think twice before you speak to a friend in need. (**Sam Goldwyn**)

Before you knock on wood, see if the doorbell works. (**Tommy Cooper**)

Chaste makes waste. (**Joan Rivers**)

If called by a panther, don't anther. (**Ogden Nash**)

Sex before marriage can be a foetal error. (**Kathy Lette**)

Love is a many gendered thing. (**Julian Cleary**)

There's nothing like an airport for bringing you down to earth. (**Richard Gordon**)

Nothing fails like failure. (**Margaret Drabble**)

Marriage is a lottery but you can't tear up your ticket if you lose. (**Milton Berle**)

Sting, where is thy death? (**Joe Queenan**)

Life's a beach. (**Pamela Anderson**)

There comes a time in every man's life when he must make way for an older man. (**Reginald Maudling**)

Love may make the world go round but it's the spinsters who oil the wheels. (**Ellen Dorothy**)

There's a great woman behind every idiot. (**John Lennon**)

Love makes time pass and time makes love pass. (**Jacques Prever**)

To the puritan all things are impure. (**D.H. Lawrence**)

The wages of sin is death but the hours are good. (**Lenny Bruce**)

I'm as pure as the driven slush. (**Tallulah Bankhead**)

Vice is its own reward. (**Quentin Crisp**)

To err is human; to forgive against company policy. (**John Goodson**)

I have an edifice complex. (**Frank Lloyd Wright**)

Some are born great, some achieve greatness, and some hire public relations officers. (**Daniel Boorstin**)

It was a game of two teams. (**Peter Brackley**)

If two wrongs don't make a right, try three. (**Arnold Wesker**)

Jack and Jill's relationship wasn't on the level. (**Sean Kilroy**)

Success is relative. The more success, the more relatives. (**Leopold Fechtner**)

A ring on the finger is worth two on the phone. (**Harold Thompson**)

First things first, but not necessarily in that order. (**Dr Who**)

Love may be the answer but while you're waiting for the answer sex raises some pretty good questions. (**Woody Allen**)

The big print giveth and the fine print taketh away. (**J. Fulton Sheen**)

By tomorrow today will be yesterday. (**Barry Scully**)

The light at the end of the tunnel is often a train coming the other way. (**Mary Beth Shank**)

Love and marriage go together like a horse and carriage but a horse and carriage is followed by manure. (**Suzanne Tumy**)

Life's a bitch – and then they call you one. (**Mary Connolly**)

We have to believe in free will. We have no choice. (**Don Crosbie**)

Overtakers keep undertakers busy. (**William Pitts**)

Women should be obscene and not heard. (**John Lennon**)

The future ain't what it used to be. (**Yogi Berra**)

Procrastinators will one day rule OK. (**Janeane Garofalo**)

Being given chances and not taking them, that's what life is all about. (**Ron Greenwood**)

If you sprinkle when you tinkle, be a sweetie and wipe the seatie. (**Eamon Holmes**)

The love that dare not speak its name is now hoarse from screaming. (**Robert Brustein**)

The old should neither be seen nor heard. (**Oscar Wilde**)

Cigarettes are the greatest known cause of statistics. (**Fletcher Knebel**)

One small step for a man, a giant taxi for Jackie Gleason. (**Jack Benny**)

Whom the mad would destroy they first make gods. (**Bernard Levin**)

New Year's Eve is where old acquaintance be forgot - unless the tests come back positive. (**Jay Leno**)

An army marches on its belly, especially if there's long grass around. (**TonyLeigh**)

A fool and his money can throw one hell of a party. (**Bob Monkhouse**)

Nothing fails like success. (**Phyllis McGinley**)

The meek may inherit the earth but they'll never increase market share. (**William McGowan**)

Once bitten, twice inoculated. (**Joe Carroll**)

Tooth will out. (**Tony Hancock**)

EC come, EC go. (**Bob Geldof**)

Run That By Me Again

In married life three is company and two is none. (**Oscar Wilde**)

All work and no play means a dramatist has Writer's Block. (**Shane O'Brien**)

My art belongs to dada. (**Cole Porter**)

Buggers can't be choosers. (**Maurice Bowra**)

The young you will always have with you. (**Don Hogan**)

Love may make the world go round but it doesn't do it half as fast as whiskey. (**Compton McKenzie**)

'I think, therefore I am' is the statement of an intellectual who under-rates toothaches. (**Milan Kundera**)

The good die young because they see it's no use living if you've got to be good. (**John Barrymore**)

If you open a Pandora's Box you never know what Trojan Horses will jump out. (**Ernest Bevin**)

Serendipity means looking for a needle in a haystack and finding a farmer's daughter. (**Auberon Waugh**)

Discretion is not the better part of biography. (**Lytton Strachey**)

I'm a man more dined against than dining. (**Maurice Bowra**)

I'm on the horns of a Dalai Lama. (**Dick Vosburgh**)

Give me a home where the buffaloes roam and I'll show you a houseful of dirt. (**Marty Allen**)

The wages of gin is breath. (**Oliver Herford**)

Two's company. Three's the result. (**Les Dawson**)

Man shall not live by bread alone but too much butter causes cholesterol. (**Ralph Gleeson**)

The best way to approach a girl with a past is with a present. (**Hal Roach**)

Incest is the theory of relativity. (**Paul Shaw**)

Less isn't more. It's less. (**Martina Devlin**)

There's no fool like a learned fool. (**Frank Sheed**)

I'd prefer to have a bottle in front of me than a frontal lobotomy. (**Tom Waits**)

Live and let die. (**Ian Fleming**)

Confucius say that if man want to grow a row of corn, first he must shovel a ton of shit. (**Stephen King**)

No good deed goes unpunished. (**Oscar Wilde**)

Justice must not be seen to be done. These days it must be seen to be believed. (**J.B. Morton**)

Man is born free but everywhere is in cellular underwear. (**Jonathan Miller**)

To forgive is human, to forget divine. (**James Grand**)

I think therefore I'm unusual. (**Mort Sahl**)

A fool and his Monet are easily parted. (**Angela Simmons**)

If you're married it only takes one to make a quarrel. (**Ogden Nash**)

Lead me not into temptation. I can find the way myself. (**Rita Mae Brown**)

If at first you don't succeed, become a plagiarist. (**Tony Killeen**)

If at first you don't succeed, try reading the directions. (**Vern McLellan**)

Birds of a feather flock together. Then they crap on your car. (**Kenny Everett**)

Old golfers never die. They simply lose their drive. (**Paul Nixon**)

Give a man a fish and you feed him for a day. Give him a fishing rod and he'll probably sell it and buy some fish. (**Simon Lamb**)

You can only predict things after they happen. (**Eugene Ionesco**)

Is a fjord a Norwegian car? (**Jerry Garcia**)

When in Rome, beware of the terrible drivers. (**Philip Francis**)

In the beginning was the word. Then there were a lot more of them. (**Spike Milligan**)

In the beginning there was nothing. Then God said, 'Let there be light.' There was still nothing but you could see it a lot better. (**Ellen DeGeneres**)

God said 'Let there be light.' Lucky him. He didn't have to pay the ESB bill. (**Roy Brown**)

Yield to temptation; it may not pass your way again. (**Richard Heinlein**)

Oh what a tangled web we weave, when bras we put on to deceive. (**Leonard Lewis Levinson**)

Ashes to ashes, clay to clay; if the enemy don't get you, your own folks may. (**James Thurber**)

Early to bed, early to rise. Make sure you get out before her husband arrives. (**Wolfgang Mieder**)

Early to bed and early to rise is a sure sign you're fed up with TV. (**Bob Phillips**)

Early to bed and early to rise and the neighbours will wonder why you can't get a job with better hours. (**Louis Safian**)

Valour is the better part of discretion. (**Jack Karnehm**)

My life has been a case of wine, women and so-long. (**Dean Martin**)

Bad newts travel fast. (**John Farman**)

He hasn't a single redeeming vice. (**Oscar Wilde**)

Life doesn't imitate art. It imitates bad TV. (**Woody Allen**)

Who dares whines. (**Simon Barnes**)

It is a truth universally acknowledged that a well-dressed man in possession of a good fortune must be a thumping great crook. (**James Healy**)

A chain is only as strong as its weakest link but the weakest one is really the strongest one because it breaks all the rest. (**Simon West**)

A little yearning is a dangerous thing. (**Roger Kilroy**)

Hara kiri takes a lot of guts. (**Colin West**)

.
Jesus saves; Moses invests. (**Herb Caen**)

Children brighten up a house. They never turn the lights out. (**Ralph Bus**)

It's better to be looked over than to be overlooked. (**Mae West**)

One man's meat is another man's cholesterol. (**Gerald Kennedy**)

Never put Descartes before de Horace. (**Milton Berle**)

Orwell that ends well. (**Nigel Rees**)

Where there's a will there's a won't. (**Ambrose Bierce**)

Where there's a will there's a lawsuit. (**Oliver Hereford**)

Punctuality is the thief of time. (**Oscar Wilde**)

Lack of money is the root of all evil. (**Mark Twain**)

Poets are born not paid. (**Wilson Mizner**)

So much time, so little to do. (**Samuel Beckett**)

If it's not one thing it's your mother. (**Robin Williams**)

Live and learn but by the time you've learned it's really too late to live. (**Carolyn Wells**)

Most of today's news is too true to be good. (**Stan Finnigan**)

Getting old means you can't take yes for an answer. (**Bob Hope**)

A boy's best friend is his mutter. (**Michael Noonan**)

If the meek do inherit the earth it's only because they wouldn't have the nerve to refuse it. (**Jackie Vernon**)

The Bible tells us to forgive our enemies. It doesn't say anything about our friends. (**Margot Asquith**)

Charity begins at home - and usually ends there too. (**Austin O'Malley**)

Beggars can't be boozers. (**John B. Keane**)

Save for a rainy day. If you can't do that, buy an umbrella. (**Jack Cruise**)

I dropped the soap in the bathroom. That's Lifebuoy. (**Tommy Cooper**)

God give me patience - but make it fast. (**TommyCooper**)

If you can't stand the heat in the dressing-room, get out of the kitchen. (**Terry Venables**)

Anyone who says talk is cheap never spoke to a tax consultant. (**Jackie Mason**)

Tony Benn immatures with age. (**Harold Wilson**)

That's Not The Way I Heard It

The saying that beauty is only skin deep is a skin deep saying. (**Herbert Spencer**)

American marriages operate on the premise of Till Debt Do Us Part. (**Johnny Carson**)

Money can't buy happiness. That's why we have credit cards. (**Red Skelton**)

With fronds like these, who needs anemones? (***Finding Nemo***)

The world may be a stage but the play is badly cast. (**Oscar Wilde**)

Old MacDonald was dyslexic, E,I,E,O,I. (**Billy Connolly**)

Too many cooks spoil the figure. (**Leopold Fechtner**)

The plain shall inherit the earth. (**Graham Norton**)

Home is where the art is. (**Andy Warhol**)

Home is where the mortgage is. (**Gideon Wurdz**)

Gentlemen prefer blondes - especially gentlemen who are married to brunettes. (**Oscar Levant**)

Early to rise and early to bed makes a man healthy, wealthy and dead. (**James Thurber**)

Time wounds all heels. (**Jane Ace**)

Gentlemen prefer bonds. (**Andrew Mellon**)

All work and no play makes Jack's wife a very wealthy widow. (**Tom McDermott**)

Time is money, especially if you buy her a Rolex. (**Arnold Palmer**)

Hate makes the world go round. (**Morrissey**)

Blood is thicker than water and also much more difficult to get out of the carpet. (**Woody Allen**)

Truth is stranger than science fiction. (**Steven Spielberg**)

Constipation is the thief of time. (**Maureen Potter**)

A pleasure shared is a pleasure halved. (**Kenneth Tynan**)

Honesty is the best policy but fire insurance pays more. (**Sid Caesar**)

Honesty is the best policy but telling a lie is probably the second best one. (**Mort Sahl**)

Fear thy neighbour as thyself. (**Eugene O'Neill**)

Mary had a little lamb. The doctor shot the shepherd. (**Roy Brown**)

A fool and his money are soon elected. (**David Southwell**)

Dyslexia means never having to say you're syrro. (**Billy Connolly**)

An *oeuf* is as good as a feast. (**Clement Freud**)

Rome wasn't built in a day, but then again I wasn't on that job. (**Brian Behan**)

Love and marriage go together like angel cake and anthrax. (**Julie Birchill**)

Tell the truth and shame the family. (**Ethel Watts Mumford**)

Home is where the heartache is. (**Kathy Lette**)

Girls just want to have funds. (**Adrienne Gusoff**)

The late bird gets the worm. The early one is usually too knackered. (**Graham Hogarth**)

A fool and her money are soon courted. (**Helen Rowland**)

To air is human, to forklift divine. (**Graham Sharkey**)

Curiosity killed the cat. I'd like to know what it was curious about. (**Michael Redmond**)

Money is the root of all evil but the foliage is fascinating. (**Val Peters**)

I sell, therefore I am. You buy, therefore I eat. (**Craig Dormanen**)

Nouveau is better than no *riche* at all. (**Eric Marc**)

Blood isn't thicker than money. (**Groucho Marx**)

A dollar saved is a quarter earned. (**John Ciardi**)

The weather is here. Wish you were beautiful. (**Ronnie Corbett**)

Prevent truth decay – leave politics. (**Cher**)

Cleanliness is almost as bad as godliness. (**Samuel Butler**)

Anything you say may be used in Everton against you. (**John Lennon**)

People who live in glass houses shouldn't throw parties. (**Stanley Davis**)

People who live in glass houses shouldn't buy wallpaper. (**Jonathan Welby**)

People who live in glass houses should dress in the basement. (**Jim Davidson**)

People who live in stucco houses shouldn't throw quiche. (**Jack Mingo**)

Home is where the mortgage is. (**Alan Pryor**)

Don't look before you leap. It ruins the surprise. (**Kris Brand**)

The pen may be mightier than the sword but it's no match for a gun. (**Al Capone**)

If the pen is mightier than the sword I'll let you have the pen if I'm fighting you in a duel. (**Steven Wright**)

We made too many wrong mistakes. (**Yogi Berra**)

Deep down I'm rather shallow. (**Charlie Haughey**)

It's as hard for a rich man to enter the kingdom of heaven as it is for a poor man to get out of Purgatory. (**Finley Peter Dunne**)

The sins of the father are often visited upon the son-in-law. (**Joan Kiser**)

Anything worth doing well is worth doing slowly. (**Gypsy Rose Lee**)

Anything worth doing has probably already been done by someone else. (**Louis Berman**)

The tedium is the message. (**Brian Eno**)

I think, therefore Descartes is. (**Saul Steinberg**)

All men are born equal but quite a few eventually get over it. (**Lord Mancroft**)

My motto is 'Veni, Vidi, Visa'. I came, I saw, I went shopping. (**Sally Poplin**)

On the other hand, you have five fingers, (**Steven Wright**)

First things first. Second things never. (**Shirley Conran**)

Too much of a good thing is wonderful. (**Liberace**)

Don't put all your eggs in one basket. Use an incubator instead. (**Gideon Wurdz**)

Give a man a fish and you feed him for a day. Teach him how to fish and you get rid of him all weekend. (**Zenna Schaffer**)

Opportunity knocks but if you have a bell it's probably better. (**Sid Caesar**)

Opportunity knocked but my doorman threw him out. (**Adrienne Gusoff**)

The chief causes of problems are solutions. (**Eric Sevareid**)

Seeing is deceiving. It's eating that's believing. (**James Thurber**)

It matters not whether you win or lose. What matters is whether I win or lose. (**Darrin Weinberg**)

He who lives by the sword will eventually be wiped out by some bastard with a sawn-off shotgun. (**Steady Eddie**)

Experience teaches that it doesn't. (**Norman McCaig**)

Opportunity only knocks once. If there's a second knock it's probably a Jehovah's Witness. (**Henny Youngman**)

To err is Truman. (**Graffiti**)

The only way to make ends meet is to burn a candle at both of them. (**Somerset Maugham**)

My wife and I have enjoyed forty years of wedded blitz. (**Hugh Leonard**)

I think, therefore I'm single. (**Liz Winstead**)

Not all dumbs are blonde. (**Mitchell Symons**)

Beauty comes from within. From within bottles, tubes and jars. (**Joan Rivers**)

A novel should have a beginning, a muddle and an end. (**Philip Larkin**)

Time flies when you're doing all the talking. (**Henny Youngman**)

He who hesitates before he leaps is lost. (**Milton Berle**)

Some things have got to be believed to be seen. (**Ralph Hodgson**)

One tequila, two tequila, three tequila, floor. (**Keith Richards**)

Eat, drink and re-marry. (**Zsa Zsa Gabor**)

Life is one canned thing after another. (**Robert Benchley**)

I'm on the horns of a Dalai Lama. (**Dick Vosburgh**)

Make love not war. I'm married so I do both. (**Rodney Dangerfield**)

Gather ye autographs while ye may. (**Cole Porter**)

If you want to make an omelette you have to turn on the microwave. (**Barbara Carson**)

He who laughs, lasts. (**Mary Pettibone Poole**)

Now is the winter of our discontent made glorious summer by central heating. (**Jack Sharkey**)

Laugh and the world laughs with you. Cry and you have to blow your nose. (**Doug Platt**)

We'll cross that bridge when we fall off it. (**Lester Pearson**)

England bowed out of the World Cup last night with their heads held high. (**Bruce Millington**)

Raquel Welch is a moron with less on. (**Totie Fields**)

Marilyn Monroe was a vacuum with nipples. (**Otto Preminger**)

I just want to be normally insane. (**Marlon Brando**)

I'm speaking off the cuff of my head. (**John Kushner**)

I can see the carrot at the end of the tunnel. (**Stuart Pearse**)

I know how hard it is to put food on your family. (**George Bush**)

The darkest hour is just before the pawn. (**Brendan Behan**)

Ian Pearce has limped off with what appears to be a shoulder injury. (**Tony Cottee**)

Chile have three options. They could win or they could lose. (**Kevin Keegan**)

Wine improves with age. The older I get, the better I like it. (**Raymond George**)

Familiarity breeds attempt. (**Goodman Ace**)

Money can't buy poverty. (**Joe E. Lewis**)

Two is company. Three is fifty bucks. (**Joan Rivers**)

If the shoe fits it's probably too expensive. (**Adrienne Gusoff**)

Where there's a will I want to be in it. (**Spike Milligan**)

What can't be cured must be insured. (**Jackie Mason**)

The pen is pointier than the sword. (**Donal Elman**)

Clones are people two. (**Diane Ward**)

Where there's smoke there's dinner. (**Jackie Gleason**)

The darkest hour is just before the dawn so if you're going to steal your neighbour's milk that's the time to do it. (**Alexei Sayle**)

Where there's smoke there's pollution. (**Kenny Everett**)

A patient without health insurance keeps the doctor away. (**Robert Vasselli**)

Daddy wouldn't buy me a Bauhaus. (**Joan Sloan**)

Where there's a will there's a dead person. (**Fred Allen**)

Two can live as cheaply as one if one doesn't eat. (**Gene Perret**)

Hull is other people. (**Jonathan Cecil**)

What's sauce for the goose is propaganda. (**Ogden Nash**)

The tide is very much in our court now. (**Kevin Keegan**)

Taste makes waist. (**James Oliver**)

No news is good news. No journalists, even better. (**Frank Sinatra**)

He who courts and does not wed may have to go to court instead. (**Evan Esar**)

Life begins at forty but so does rheumatism. (**Rodney Dangerfield**)

All's well that ends. (**Herb Ansell**)

Afterword

If you enjoyed reading these thoughts half as much as I enjoyed writing them, that means I will have enjoyed writing them twice as much as you enjoyed reading them.